A gift for:

_____

From:

_____

Life Wisdom
— from —
Coach
WOODEN

GIFT BOOKS
from Hallmark

Editorial Director: Todd Hafer
Editing and Compilation by The DesignWorks Group, Sisters, OR
Art Director: Kevin Swanson
Designer/Production Artist: Dan Horton

Printed and bound in China
ISBN: 978-1-59530-139-0

First Edition, March 2008
11 10 9 8 7 6 5 4 3 2

BOK5529

Contents

Introduction

They call him Coach. Just Coach. For a two-time Hall of Famer with ten national championships, two Coach of the Century awards, and the Presidential Medal of Honor under his belt, it is a title that John Wooden has most definitely earned after eight decades on the basketball court — decades that included being a star player as well as a legendary coach. At Indiana's Martinsville High, he was a three-time all-state guard who led his team to a state title and two second place finishes.

Then at Purdue University, he was a three-time All-America guard who led the Boilermakers to two Big 10 titles and a national championship (in 1932). He also lettered in baseball — as a freshman.

Today, as he approaches his 100th birthday, Coach Wooden continues to be the best he can be. He has written three successful books in the past decade and continues to speak across the country. He also keeps in touch with many of his former players, who revere him. "To play for John Wooden," noted basketball legend Bill Walton, "was the greatest thrill of my life. In four years, Wooden taught us everything we'd ever need to know. Not about basketball, about life."

But while most people know him as the most

honored collegiate basketball coach in history, John Wooden came from humble and simple beginnings. He grew up on a farm, where his parents taught their children to live lives of deep faith in God. That is the driving force behind Coach's life purpose — to model Jesus Christ in all he does. Personal integrity is his highest goal.

This book is a compilation of some of Coach Wooden's most memorable words. From the keys to personal and professional success, to keeping life's priorities straight, to the importance of hard work, Coach shares the wisdom only someone of his experience and lifelong learning could deliver. Read on, and be coached by the best!

On Being a

True Leader

A

leader's most
powerful ally
is his or her
own example.

The most important profession in the world is parenting. The second is teaching, and everyone is a teacher to someone.

I'm convinced that regardless of task, leaders must be enthusiastic and really enjoy what they're doing if they expect those under their supervision to work near their respective levels of competency. With few exceptions, an unenthusiastic leader will keep those under his or her charge from achieving their collective best.

We don't have to be superstars or win championships.... All we have to do is learn to rise to every occasion, give our best effort, and make those around us better as we do it.

Leadership from a base of hypocrisy undermines respect, and if people don't respect you, they won't willingly follow you.

Approval is a greater motivator than disapproval, but we have to disapprove on occasion when we correct. It's necessary. I make corrections only after I have proved to the individual that I highly value him. If they know we care for them, our correction won't be seen as judgmental. I also try to never make it personal.

Be slow to correct and quick to commend.

I never yelled at my players much.
That would have been artificial stimulation, which doesn't last very long.
I think it's like love and passion.
Passion won't last as long as love.
When you are dependent on passion, you need more and more of it to make it work.
It's the same with yelling.

Sometimes when I overheard one of my players use profanity during practice, I would dismiss him for the day. My boys all knew that practice was where they earned their playing time, so I used the sessions themselves as a disciplinary measure. If anyone cursed during a game, I would sit him on the bench for a while. It didn't take long for my players to clean up their language. There was not trash talk on my teams.

Once,
one of my players
was asked
if I ever used
profanity.
"Absolutely,"
he replied.
"'Goodness, gracious,
sakes alive'
is profanity for Coach."

I was a stickler
for time management
almost from the beginning.
With me, being on time was,
and still is, vital.
Nonetheless,
in my early days of teaching,
sometimes when things
weren't going well,
I kept my team longer.
This was counterproductive.
I learned
that when players are tired
physically,
they are usually tired
mentally as well.
It took me too long to learn
that this does not
lead to [efficiency].

When a person changes, he or she usually ends up with a feeling of superiority. I didn't want that to happen to my players, and I didn't want it to happen to me. I was flattered when one of the coaches at the NCAA convention introduced me by saying, "John is no different after winning ten championships than before he won one." That made me feel good, because I want to practice what I teach.

On Living With
Integrity

Honest people
don't lie
to others,
to themselves,
or to God.

The five people
who first come to mind
that best reflect
the quality
of integrity
are Jesus,
my dad,
Abraham Lincoln,
Mother Teresa,
and Billy Graham.
The order of the last three
really doesn't matter.

Purity of intention is really a reflection of the heart, and having a pure heart is so important....The heart of a person with integrity always wants to do what's right, once he or she is sure what "right" is.

Your reputation is what you're perceived to be. Your character is what you really are.

I believe in the value of loyalty.

I do not have a problem

with an NBA player

requesting a contract extension

or a renegotiation,

but to threaten

to not give his best

if his contract isn't changed

(as has happened)

compromises his integrity.

It's not right.

There is something wrong

when your loyalty

is always available

to the highest bidder.

Being true to ourselves doesn't make us people of integrity. Charles Manson was true to himself, and as a result, he rightly is spending the rest of his life in prison. Ultimately, being true to our Creator gives us the purest form of integrity.

I've never stopped trying to do what's right. I'm not doing it to earn favor with God. I'm doing it because it's the right thing to do.

Honesty
is not only
the best policy, but
it is also
the best therapy.
Telling the truth
and being true
to ourselves
not only enhances
our relations with others
and with God,
but it also
makes us feel good
about ourselves.

I believe we are most likely to succeed when ambition is focused on noble and worthy purposes and outcomes rather than on goals set out of selfishness.

In every championship game when we had the game won, during a time-out, I directed the players, "Don't make fools out of yourselves. Let's let the alumni and the fans do that. I know you want to get the nets, and I know you feel good, and that's fine, but let's have no excessive exultation." Each of my championship teams won with class, and I'm proud of that.

I wanted my players to always be searching, especially for truth. I wanted them to know what they believed and be able to defend it. Truth will always stand the test of scrutiny.

Some evangelical Christians
think of me
as being liberal
because they disagree
with my decision
to let my life
speak for my faith.
At the same time,
liberals
consider me to be
way too conservative.
I know
you can't please everyone,
so on this issue,
I haven't tried.
I have only wanted
to please God.

If I did only
what I wanted to do,
I would not be obedient
to the Creator.
Sometimes He wants us
to do certain things
that we may not
feel like doing.
When it comes
to what God asks of us,
we need more than
good intentions – we need
to follow through fully.

The Rewards of
Hard Work

There is no substitute for work. Worthwhile results come from hard work and careful planning.

Time lost is time lost.
It's gone forever.
Some people tell themselves
that they will work
twice as hard tomorrow
to make up for
what they did not do today.
People should always do their best.
If they can work
twice as hard tomorrow,
then they should have also worked
twice as hard today.
That would have been their best.
Catching up
leaves no room for them
to do their best tomorrow.
People with the philosophy
of putting off and then
working twice as hard
cheat themselves.

We almost have to
force or drive ourselves
to work hard
if we are to reach
our potential.
If we don't enjoy
what we do,
we won't be able
to push as hard
as we need to push
for as long
as we need to push
to achieve our best.
However,
if we enjoy
what we do
and if we're enthusiastic
about it,
we'll do it better
and come closer
to becoming
the best we can be.

Undirected diligence isn't very **efficient;** therefore, an element of **planning** must go into **hard work.**

The maxim
"easy come, easy go"
carries more truth in
it than most people
realize. When we
add to our
accomplishments
the element
of hard work over a
long period of time,
we'll place a far greater
value on the outcome.
When we are patient,
we'll have a greater
appreciation of
our success.

I must have the drive
to develop my abilities
and become
the best I can be
so that I'll be ready.
If I'm prepared,
perhaps my chance will come.
But if I'm not primed,
I'll miss my opportunity,
and it isn't likely to come again.
I have to think
as if I'm only going
to get one shot,
so I must be ready.

The best competition
I have is against
myself to
become
better.

Make no mistake;

I always want to win,

but I never fight

with an opponent.

My fight is within me —

it is the struggle

to be the best

I can be

at whatever I do.

On
Working
Together

Kindness makes for much better teamwork.

God created us to be interdependent. We were not designed to go through life alone. We become so much more when we come alongside others—and we make them better, too.

In the sixth game of
the 1998 NBA finals,
Michael Jordan had
the flu, yet he played.
During time-outs,
toward the end of the
game, he would almost
pass out, yet he contin-
ued. When he finally won
the game, scoring his for-

ty-fifth point of the game with 5.2 seconds to go, he could no longer stand; his teammates had to hug him while he was seated. He was completely spent—he had left it all on the floor— but he had willed his team to play their best.

When you
are a member
of a **team,**
you do everything
as a team.
One of my players
once gave me
a great **compliment.**
He said,
"Coach Wooden
doesn't **see** race.
He's just looking
for players
who will **play** together."
Hearing that
gave me about
as **good** a feeling
as I could ever have.

We can become great

in the eyes of others,

but we'll never become successful

when we compromise our character

and show disloyalty

toward friends or teammates.

The reverse is also true:

No individual or team

will become great without loyalty.

When we perform a task that we *should or must* do for the good of the group, our heart isn't completely in it. This slight reluctance holds back our teammates. By contrast, when every member of a team eagerly performs every task, the group rises to a new level of accomplishment.

A
Healthy
Perspective

Concentrate on what you

do have,

not on what you don't.

Regarding balance—

it's the most important

component in basketball

and it is a very important

part of life.

We must always

keep things in perspective

so that we can

maintain emotional control.

Time spent getting even would be better spent getting ahead.

Good things take time, as they should. We shouldn't expect good things to happen overnight. Actually, getting something too easily or too soon can cheapen the outcome.

We are all equal

in that we can

all strive to become

the best we are capable of becoming.

We can always improve,

but we shouldn't

compare ourselves to others.

We get in trouble

when we start trying

to measure up

to someone else.

I

[am] sure God hears
all of our prayers
and answers them—
but sometimes
the answer is no.

I don't think we are supposed to find our own truth. That's playing God. I believe in absolute truth and absolute sin, and the Bible is my standard for determining those absolutes. With that in mind, I believe that an inquisitive person is more apt to discover truth than someone with a closed mind.

Keeping Priorities Straight

Don't let

making a living

prevent you

from making a life.

People don't spend enough time with their families. They get caught up in material things, thinking that those make up life. The pursuit of material possessions often takes precedence over the things that are more lasting, such as faith, family, and friends. Don't allow the lesser values to wreak havoc on your family.

Earlier in life, I put family in front of faith. I've fixed that. But I always tried to keep work fourth on the list. I was proud when [my wife] Nellie told an interviewer, "I never could tell whether John had a good practice or a bad practice, because he never brought it home."

I know
church attendance alone
does not
make a person
a Christian.
It takes
a personal relationship
with our Creator,
which comes about
only through
God's grace.

In 1943,
a friend gave me a small cross,
and I've carried it in a pocket ever since.
It's not a good luck charm
or anything like that,
but I held it in my hand
during games,
and I still grab it
during times of tension.
It reminds me
who is in control
and who I represent.
It probably is a good thing for officials
that I had that
in my hand
when a bad call was made.
Although the phrase
was not in vogue back then,
in a way,
the cross in my pocket
spoke to me and asked
"What would Jesus do?"
in any particular situation.

I [always] felt that
if [the players] were
fully prepared,
we would do
just fine.
If we won, great—
frosting on the cake.
But at no time
did I consider
winning
to be the cake.
Winning has always
been the frosting
that made the cake
a little tastier.

When we have

prioritize the

As a result, peo

goals tend

team and oth

them while

the Pyramid

noble goals, we

bigger picture.

ble with noble

to bring the

rs along with

they climb

of Success.

Everyone wants to do as much as one can for one's family. However, if a person gets too focused on material things, he or she will forget the more lasting things. All material assets, in one way or another, will go away. I really believe that happiness comes from things that cannot be taken away from you.

I never encouraged
anyone to pray for a win.
I don't think our prayers
should be directed
to the score of a game.
That seems way too selfish.
I wanted my boys
to honor God
by doing their best,
controlling their emotions,
and asking for protection.
Those are the good requests
for basketball players
and for our lives in general.

On
Being Kind

There is nothing stronger than gentleness.

Love your fellow man.

It's the second commandment.

I know we are

to love God first,

but we must also

not forget

to love each other.

People will always
have problems,
but I don't think
any problem
is unmanageable
if each side is
more considerate
of the other.
We must not force
our feelings onto others,
and we must
accept the fact
that there can
be differences.

"The worst things you can do for the ones you love are the things they could and should do for themselves." I think Lincoln said it first— I'm not sure—but I've used it so much over the years that the saying has become a part of me. I've used it a lot because I believe it deeply.

Friendship

is doing for others

while they are doing for you.

It's called ministry

when all of the doing

goes in one direction.

Friendship goes both ways.

Friendship is like a good marriage—

it's based on mutual concern.

Friends help each other;

they don't use each other.

Sincerity
may not help us
make friends,
but it will help us
keep them.

We can give without loving, but we can't love without giving. In fact, love is nothing unless we give it to someone.

There is always great joy in learning that something you've said or done has been meaningful to another, especially when you do it without any thought of receiving anything in return. Your gift doesn't even have to be material. Helping others in any way—with a smile, a nod, or a pat on the back—warms the heart.

There is a wonderful axiom
about the three things
most people really want
out of life:
happiness,
freedom,
and peace of mind.
Interestingly,
these things
are usually attained
when we give them away. When we are
fortunate enough
to have them,
the three are also
a form of shelter.
The life we lead
and the friends we make
can be shelters, too.

Surviving the
Tough Times

Some of my greatest pleasures have come from finding ways to overcome obstacles.

We're all imperfect, and we all have needs. The weak usually do not ask for help, so they stay weak. If we recognize that we are imperfect, we will ask for help and we will pray for the guidance necessary to bring positive results to whatever we are doing.

As I entered adulthood, I faced the same kind of challenges my folks had faced, and I quickly had to learn to get along with very little. A few days before Nellie and I were to be married, a bank failure took my life savings of $909.05, which was a lot of money in those days. A friend loaned us some cash so that we could get married anyway. I left to fight in World War II, and when I returned, another financial problem awaited me: The bank had foreclosed on our home. My parents had shown me how to handle the setback, so we packed up and moved on. When I was on staff at Indiana State University, I was director of athletics, head basketball and baseball coach, and taught courses. I also worked to finish my master's thesis. I look back and think, How could I possibly have done all of that! But I had not thought of it as a hardship at the time, and I never made excuses.

I've always taught the **importance** of keeping our **emotions** under **control,** but we must deal with grief when it comes. Grief **controlled** me for a season, and that's **natural,** I suppose. When grief passed, so did the **questions.** I was able to get back to the **reality** that God is far **greater** than I am and to see that I must **accept** His **actions,** even if I do not **understand** them at the time.

Do not permit what you cannot do to interfere with what you can do.

We can plan
a road trip
or a workday
down to the last detail,
but the unexpected
will always arise.
If we are not
malleable,
we will get left behind.

We don't start
with calculus;
we start with arithmetic.
After we learn the basics,
we move on to algebra,
then to geometry,
and so on.
We work our way
up to calculus.
In the same way,
we grow stronger spiritually
through the tests of life.

Let's face it, we're all imperfect and we're going to fall short on occasion, but we must learn from failure, and that will enable us to avoid repeating our mistakes. Through adversity, we learn, grow stronger, and become better people.

The more concerned

we become over

the things

we can't control,

the less we will do

with the things

we can control.

On
Finding Success

Failure is not fatal,
but failure to change
can be.

This is my life's most defining maxim: Success is peace of mind as a direct result of self-satisfaction in knowing that you did your best to become the best that you are capable of becoming – in all areas of life.

In life,

worthwhile accomplishments

and acquisitions

take time.

Usually the better

the reward,

the more time

it takes to acquire it.

We should never let ambition cause us to sacrifice our integrity or diminish our efforts in other [areas]. However, we need to remember that we never reach a serious goal unless we have the intention of doing so.

Remember,
results aren't the criteria
for success—
it's the effort
made for
achievement
that is most important.

The person who is afraid to risk failure seldom has to face success. I expected my players to make mistakes, as long as they were mistakes of commission. A mistake of commission happens when you are doing what should be done but don't get the results you want.

When we are

miss opportuni

ourselves. We

watch for cir

or situations that

us and be ea

from these

n't alert, we

ties to improve

should always

cumstances

can help or harm

ger to learn

encounters.

To become our best, good judgment and common sense are essential. No matter the task—whether physical or mental— if our emotions take over, we're not going to execute near our personal level of competency, because both judgment and common sense will be impaired. When our emotions domi- nate our actions, we make mistakes.

Each of us has a huge capacity to learn and to achieve. Being ever alert makes the task of becoming all we are capable of becoming so much easier.

You may be better than the rest, but you are not a success until you have made the effort to become the best you can be.

Players with fight
never lose
a game;
they just run
out of time.

If we fail to adapt,
  we fail to move forward.

Although there is no progress without change, not all change is progress.

To achieve significance,

it's a good idea

to select an activity

for which God

has given us

at least

a measure of skill.

Physical conditioning

is important....

But a failure to address

mental,

moral,

and spiritual

conditioning

will limit even the best

physical conditioning.

Those who primarily work alone will never become all they could become if they were working with others. Working with others makes us much more than we could ever become alone.

.

God made only one Lewis Alcindor
(a.k.a. Kareem Abdul-Jabbar),
one Billy Graham....
The rest of us
didn't receive as much potential
as the highest achievers,
but each of us
can still become successful.
We might not become
as significant
as we aspire to be,
but we can become
the best we are capable of becoming.

You can make mistakes and not be a failure if you give it your full effort. Effort includes both preparation and execution. You are never a failure if you gave it your all, unless you blame others for your mistakes. When you place blame, you're making excuses; when you're making excuses, you can't evaluate yourself; and without self-evaluation, failure is inevitable.

You
are the only one
who knows
whether you have
won.

Wooden on
Himself

If I am ever
through
learning,
I am
through.

While I am losing my abilities
and technology has zoomed past me,
I'm not going to get upset.
It's the natural, normal way of life.
I will continue
to do the best
with what I have.

I grew up on a farm. We learned that there was a season to plant, a season to water, and a season to harvest. The planting and watering could be laborious, but without those stages, there would never be a harvest.

I never tried to change
a person's faith.
I saw that
as God's job,
not mine.
I did encourage my players
to stay open-minded,
however,
because I felt
that those who were
open-minded
would give way to truth
and those who weren't
wouldn't.
I have always believed
that what Christ said is truth,
and that He is Truth.

When we were growing up
on the farm,
every night
[my father]
would read to us
from the Scriptures and poetry.
To this day,
I usually read
my Bible
a couple of times a day,
and I still enjoy
attempting to express
my feelings
through poetry.

It is very difficult to be successful without a strong sense of spiritual well-being. I believe God wants us to be strong in our faith. Jesus said to seek Him first and then He would add all things. I have sought Him first and foremost, and I have tried to do my best. I am at peace.

As I grow older, I appreciate things that I didn't appreciate much when I was younger. I am thankful more than I used to be. I've been reasonably healthy, and I feel blessed. And each morning I can think, this is going to be a good day!

Bibliography

Content for this book was gleaned from
the following sources:

*Coach Wooden One-on-One: Inspiring
Conversations on Purpose, Passion and the
Pursuit of Success* by John Wooden and
Jay Carty. Copyright 2003 by John Wooden
and Jay Carty. Used by permission of
Regal Books from Gospel Light.

*Coach Wooden's Pyramid of Success:
Building Blocks for a Better Life* by John
Wooden; Jay Carty. Copyright 2005 by

If you have enjoyed this book,
Hallmark would love
to hear from you.

Please send your comments to

Book Feedback
Hallmark Cards, Inc.
2501 McGee, Mail Drop 215
Kansas City, MO 64108

Or email us at
booknotes@hallmark.com